Cycles of Nature

Life Cycles

by Jaclyn Jaycox

Raintree is an imprint of Capstone Global Library Limited, a company incorporated
in England and Wales having its registered office at 264 Banbury Road, Oxford, OX2
7DY – Registered company number: 6695582

www.raintree.co.uk
myorders@raintree.co.uk

Editor: Alesha Sullivan
Designer: Charmaine Whitman
Media Researcher: Morgan Walters
Production Specialist: Katy LaVigne

ISBN 978 1 4747 9517 3 (hardback)
ISBN 978 1 4747 9529 6 (paperback)

British Library Cataloguing in Publication Data
A full catalogue record for this book is available from the British Library.

Acknowledgements
Shutterstock: Anita Kainrath, 13, Ann Marie Walkington, 5, Anton_Ivanov, (left)
Cover, Bogdan Wankowicz, 15, cynoclub, 21, GraphicsRF, 17, MZPHOTO.CZ,
(bottom) Cover, Rich Carey, 19, Sergey 402, (egg) Cover, Toluk, (circles) design
element throughout, vkilikov, 11, vladsilver, 7, 9

Printed in India
983

Contents

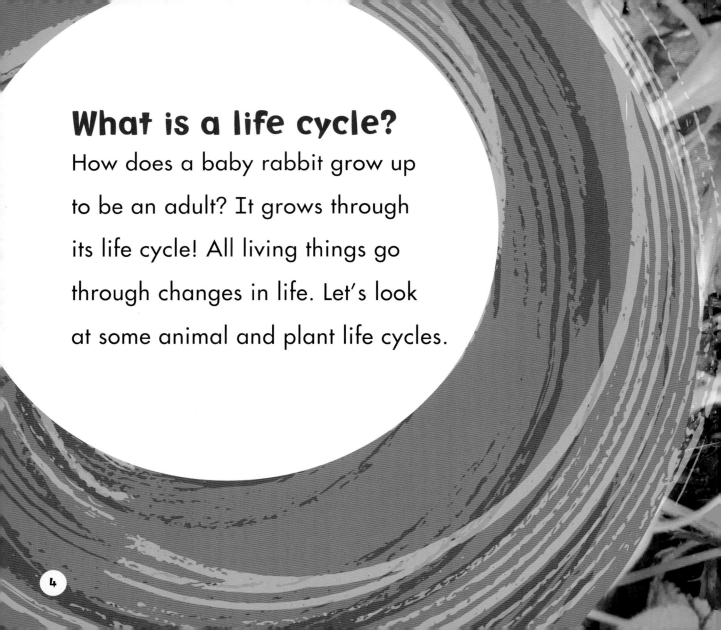

What is a life cycle?

How does a baby rabbit grow up to be an adult? It grows through its life cycle! All living things go through changes in life. Let's look at some animal and plant life cycles.

Emperor penguins

An emperor penguin begins life in an egg. The male penguin keeps the egg warm. The penguin chick hatches after about two months. The male and female feed the chick and keep it warm.

After about one year, the parents leave the chick. Now it can swim and hunt for itself. It can have a baby of its own. Emperor penguins live for about 20 years.

Dolphins

A female bottlenose dolphin gives birth to a baby. The baby dolphin is called a calf. It drinks milk from its mother.

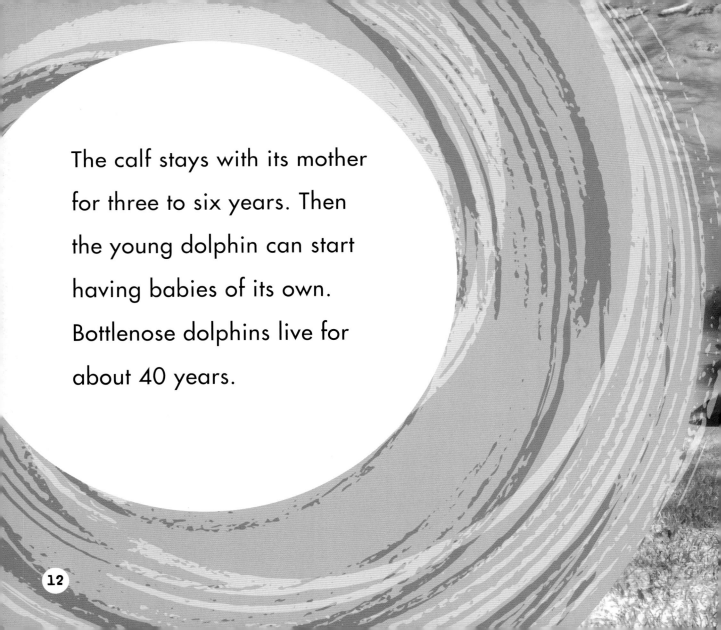

The calf stays with its mother for three to six years. Then the young dolphin can start having babies of its own. Bottlenose dolphins live for about 40 years.

Sunflowers

A sunflower starts as a tiny seed in the soil. Sunshine and rain help the seed to grow roots. Then a shoot comes up out of the ground. Then leaves start to grow.

15

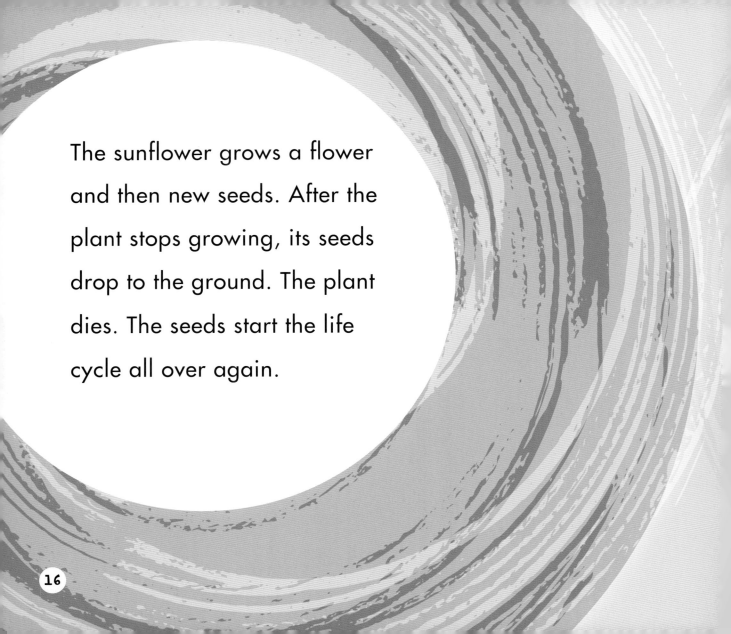

The sunflower grows a flower and then new seeds. After the plant stops growing, its seeds drop to the ground. The plant dies. The seeds start the life cycle all over again.

Sunflower life cycle

People and life cycles

Life cycles repeat. But people's actions can make it hard for some plants and animals to live. People cut down forests to build new towns. Some animals lose their homes.

Sometimes people hunt when they shouldn't. Many animals can't repeat their life cycle. We can help. We can protect plants and animals.

Glossary

calf a baby dolphin

hatch to break out of an egg

life cycle the series of changes that take place in a living thing, from birth to death

root part of a plant that grows under the ground and takes in water

seed the part of a flower that will grow into a new plant

shoot the stem growing out of a seed that becomes a plant

Find out more

A Butterfly's Life Cycle (Explore Life Cycles), Mary Dunne (Raintree, 2017)

A Sunflower's Life Cycle (Explore Life Cycles), Mary Dunne (Raintree, 2017)

Life Cycles (Earth by Numbers), Nancy Dickmann (Raintree, 2019)

Websites

BBC Bitesize: The Life Cycle of Animals
www.bbc.co.uk/bitesize/topics/z6882hv/articles/zttckqt

BBC Bitesize: What is a Life Cycle?
www.bbc.co.uk/bitesize/topics/zgssgk7/articles/zwn6mnb

National Geographic Kids: The Butterfly Life Cycle
www.natgeokids.com/nz/discover/animals/insects/butterfly-life-cycle/

Comprehension questions

1. Emperor penguins lay eggs. What other animals can you think of that also lay eggs? What do they have in common?

2. How else do you think people might affect plant and animal life cycles?

Index